Saturdays. There are also numerous antique shops, which have gained Ely an enviable reputation in this field.

Visitors coming to Ely for the first time are invariably surprised that such a small place has so much to offer. The magnificent Cathedral is surrounded by attra[...] buildings, there are [...] museums, a pictures[...] and surrounding cou[...] own unique appeal.

The people of Ely [...] independenc[...] from the days of the Anglo-Saxon hero Hereward the Wake, and when teased about the flatness of their landscape they reply that any fool can enjoy mountain scenery, but it takes a person of discernment to appreciate the fens.

[...] now there is a flea-market held in the Market Place on Saturdays as well.

FRONT COVER
Clockwise from the top right: Oliver Cromwell; Steeple Gate; the riverside and Cathedral; Oliver Cromwell's House; an Ely sunset; the west front of Ely Cathedral.

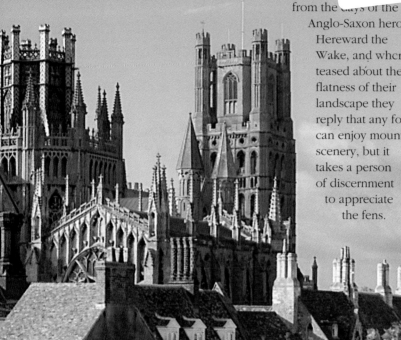

This impressive reconstruction of the Roman building found at Stonea – probably a procurator's villa – is in the Ely Museum. It was a two- or three-storey tower with a glazed and richly decorated hall heated by hypocaust. Roads radiated into the countryside from the complex, which must have served as the hub of regional administration and defences for about 100 years until it was demolished early in the 3rd century.

History

The first evidence of settlement in the fens comes from around 4300BC with the discovery of flint weapons and tools. After a rise in sea-level caused the flooding of the fenland basin, deposits of peat began to be laid down as vegetation decayed.

When the Romans reached the fens around AD100, they found a wilderness of marsh and water. They disliked areas where insurgents could hide, so throughout their occupation they attempted to build causeways and canals to improve communications. It has been suggested that the Romans may well have annexed the fens as an imperial estate, an idea partly confirmed by the recent discovery of the foundations of a large building at Stonea which could have served to administer the district. The fens would thus have been a preserved area dedicated to hunting and agriculture with restricted access making it difficult for anti-Roman forces to operate.

During the Dark Ages roads, canals and drainage cuts made by the Romans fell into disrepair, a process aided by a further rise in sea-level. Vikings frequently sailed up the rivers and raided the small communities, though they could seldom have found much worth keeping.

At the beginning of the 7th century East Anglia was ruled by King Anna, father of St Etheldreda, who with his daughter became an early convert to Christianity. Although Etheldreda made clear her preference for a life dedicated to Christ, two political marriages were forced upon her. In 652 she was married to Tondbert, a powerful local prince. He died after three years and soon afterwards Etheldreda married again, this time to Egfrith, a child-prince from Northumbria. One of the conditions of the marriage, as with the previous one, was that it should be unconsummated. However, when he grew older, Egfrith, by now the king, had a change of heart, and his queen fled to a convent at Coldingham, close to the Scottish border. After a while her husband learned of her whereabouts and Etheldreda had to flee again, eventually reaching the Isle of Ely.

Etheldreda first settled at Cratendune (close to Little Thetford, just to the south of Ely) where she had founded a monastery on inheriting fenland after the death of her first husband. Etheldreda moved her priory to the hilltop site of the present Cathedral after Cratendune burned down in

RIGHT Stone coffins were used for burials in Roman times and were often reused later (St Etheldreda was reinterred in such a coffin made of white marble). This Anglo-Saxon coffin can be seen in the Ely Museum.

until being destroyed at the Reformation. On the death of Sexburga, her daughter Erminalda succeeded as abbess and queen. All three queen-abbesses were later made saints.

Etheldreda's abbey was destroyed by Vikings around 870 and its site neglected for almost 100 years before a new Benedictine monastery rose from the ruins. King Edgar sponsored the venture and appointed Æthelwold, bishop and abbot of Winchester, to raise funds for its upkeep. By the year 1000 Ely's fortunes had revived as a flourishing market town with a wealthy and powerful abbey.

King Harold appointed Thurstan, a local man, as abbot. He was instrumental in making the Isle of Ely the last region to defy the might of the Normans and was supported in this by the earls of Chester and Northumberland with Hereward the Wake (see panel on page 6), whose exploits were romanticized by Charles Kingsley in his novel *Hereward the Wake* (1866). After five years of resistance, monks betrayed Ely's defences and Anglo-Saxon resistance was broken. In 1081 Simeon, a relative of the King, was appointed abbot and, though over 80 years old, began the building of a magnificent cathedral, dedicated to God but also a symbol of Norman authority.

With stable government and the Benedictine monastery attracting

**ABOVE
St Etheldreda shown with the Cathedral in her hand – Victorian stained glass in Ely Cathedral.**

RIGHT As she fled from Northumberland, St Etheldreda fell asleep and when she woke her staff had taken root. This incident is carved in one of the capitals of the octagon.

673. As abbess, Queen Etheldreda was renowned for her piety though she only lived for six more years, dying on 23 June 679 from a throat tumour.

Etheldreda's sister, Queen Sexburga, succeeded as abbess and supervised Etheldreda's exhumation in 695, when the body was found to be perfectly preserved. Her remains were removed to a coffin of white marble, probably Roman. The reinterment or translation of Etheldreda took place on 17 October which, with 23 June, remains dedicated to her at Ely. Over the centuries her shrine was venerated for its healing properties

LEFT A photograph taken *c.* 1890 shows bundles of osiers being unloaded at Fear's Basket Works.

There are two schools of thought about Hereward ('the Wake' is a fanciful later addition to his name and means 'the Watchful'). One makes him a Robin Hood figure who defied a brutal occupying army with a handful of followers making a last-ditch effort in the watery fastness of the Isle of Ely to preserve his nation from the tyranny of William I. The other has him as an opportunistic bandit who took advantage of chaotic times to plunder church property, although allowance should be made for this version originating from the pen of a Norman monk. The truth probably lies between the two versions. (Also see page 5.)

thousands of pilgrims to the shrine of St Etheldreda, Ely began to prosper again, and by the time of the 'Domesday' survey the priory was the second-wealthiest foundation in the kingdom. Eels were the most important local commodity, and the rivers also supplied great quantities of fish, plus wildfowl and their eggs. The reedbeds gave rushes and sedge for floor-coverings and thatching. Willow withies were woven into baskets, while fishing-rods were made from alder. Peat was dug for fuel – and for primitive building – and this industry survived until reserves ran out in the

19th century. In summer herdsmen moved cattle down to the rich grass of the floodlands.

Henry I granted Ely a charter to hold a week-long fair at the festival of St Etheldreda in June. By medieval times the town had become a thriving community in the shadow of a powerful abbey, where building work continued through three centuries, attracting hundreds of craftsmen. Some worked on the monastic buildings that surrounded the Cathedral, many of which can be seen today. The medieval great hall used by the monks is now the Bishop's House, Priory

RIGHT The Prior's House (now Priory House) is part of the medieval monastery used by the King's School.

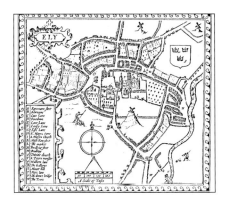

themselves for all their stilts cannot stalke through' (a reference to the stilts that were used to wade through deep water).

The district profoundly effected the Civil War since it was here that Oliver Cromwell was raised. The impressions and opinions he formed at Huntingdon and Ely became revolutionary beliefs that were to change the course of British history. Cromwell's influence saved Ely Cathedral from damage by iconoclasts. He strongly disapproved of music in church and in 1644 was angered when his request for the choir to be disbanded was ignored. At the next opportunity he attended service with his supporters and forced the stubborn canon and the congregation out of the Cathedral, locked the door and pocketed the key. It remained locked for 17 years.

The 18th century saw a gradual improvement in the fortunes of Ely reflected by the fine houses of the period found in the centre of the city and in the Waterside. Fenland drainage remained controversial but in many districts fen slodgers managed to cling on to the old way of life. They were a stubborn breed who

House is used by the King's School as is Prior Crauden's Chapel close by, built at much the same time as the lantern and Lady Chapel. Adjacent to the chancel of the Cathedral are the infirmary buildings, which reflect the importance of the abbey to the local community as the 60 or so monks and nuns at Ely could never have needed such extensive facilities.

Revenue from pilgrims ended with the removal of St Etheldreda's shrine at the Reformation, and the monastic buildings were incorporated into the King's New College, and these were subsequently used by the King's School. The Cathedral had its statues defaced and stained glass smashed but otherwise survived the upheaval, and its bishop remained in place, while the last prior became the first dean. At this time the population of Ely only numbered about 1700 but it was set to grow through the next century as workers were recruited to dig channels for the 'Adventurers' – wealthy landowners and London financiers who provided capital for draining the fens.

As the water drained off the surrounding countryside, access to Ely improved, and travellers began to explore the district. Early in the 17th century, Camden found fenmen 'rude, uncivil and envious to all others'. Here were 'foule and flabby quaremiles, yea and most troublesome Fennes, which the very inhabitants

RIGHT A punt-gun mounted on a sledge was a formidable weapon for a wildfowler though its recoil would be potentially perilous.

lived in damp hovels built of clay and peat. They survived by catching eels, tench and pike, which were sent to London markets in great water butts so that they would arrive fresh even after travelling for several days. Enormous decoys, owned by wealthy landlords and let out to operators for substantial annual rents, trapped hundreds of wildfowl. From St Ives alone, 6000 ducks were sent to

RIGHT The view westwards from the west tower of the Cathedral, showing the parish church and St Mary's Street.

ABOVE **Samuel and Nathaniel Buck's engraving of the south-east panorama of Ely from 1743 shows the west tower of the Cathedral with a spire.**

the Adventurers in lieu of interest. Further land previously used as common grazing was enclosed so that small farmers were dispossessed. Conditions became so bad that in 1816 a group from Littleport took up arms against the wealthy landowners. Encouraged by early success, they marched on Ely armed with billhooks and scythes and trundling a farm cart mounted with four punt-guns. The rioters met with little opposition and ransacked the houses of the rich and drank the pubs dry. The uprising was put down by the arrival of dragoons; after their intervention more than 50 rioters stood trial and five of them were hanged, the rest being imprisoned or transported.

market each week. Incessant dampness, and consequently mosquitoes, brought agues and fevers to many fenmen and gave rise to the saying:

Poppy tea and opium pill
Are the fen cure for many an ill.

The beginning of the 19th century was a bad time for agriculture and thus for Ely too. When the fens were drained the land had been given to

The railway arrived in 1845, stimulating new crops and industries. Boatbuilding was an important industry based in Babylon on the far bank of the Ouse. In 1925 a sugar-beet factory was built but closed after 50 years of production.

Since 1801 the population has grown from 4000 to 12,000, and Ely today remains a flourishing and independent city with a strong sense of local community.

RIGHT **The view looking eastwards over the lantern from the west tower of the Cathedral.**

Ely Cathedral and Precincts

ABOVE **The west tower of the Cathedral from Palace Green. The Russian cannon is in the foreground.**

The main entrance to the Cathedral is by the west door, the approach from this side passing the Russian cannon on the Green and the old Bishop's Palace to the right, now a Sue Ryder home. From this side the great western tower fills the sky and the elaborate Norman decoration of the surviving western transept is well seen. After the impressive porch (known as the Galilee in Ely, it dates from 1215 but was drastically restored by Sir George Gilbert Scott in 1847) the visitor is confronted by the breathtaking vista down the length of the nave.

Building began in 1083, starting at the east end of the church so that the choir, crossing and transepts were completed before work began on the nave. The master mason responsible for this chose to build high and narrow. Even though work on the nave must have gone on for 60 or 70 years it is all in uniform style with 24

RIGHT **The panel at the east end of the nave ceiling depicting the Adoration was painted by Thomas Gambier Parry.**

undecorated columns and plain walls. In contrast the ceiling is golden and lavishly painted with biblical scenes, the work of two gifted amateur artists in the mid-19th century. With the ceiling half completed, the original artist – Henry le Strange – died, probably from lung disease brought on by breathing fumes from the paint. He executed the Old Testament scenes lying on his back, his face only inches from the ceiling. The work was completed by his friend Thomas Parry, who painted the easternmost panels in the pre-Raphaelite style then becoming fashionable. Although the eye is drawn onwards and upwards, don't fail to look down before moving on. The floor at the west end of the nave is paved with tiles forming a maze that not only symbolises the continuity of life but also reflects the age-old belief that a maze will confuse evil spirits thinking of entering a building.

From the maze, move southwards, to the right, to look upwards at the profuse decoration of the south-west transept. The ascending orders of rounded Norman arches culminate in

a completely new style in the windows at the top, where the arches are pointed, showing that in the last phase of building, *c.* 1200, the masons adopted the new Early English style.

ABOVE **The glorious orders of Norman architecture displayed in the arcades of the south-west transept.**

LEFT **The maze at the western entrance to the Cathedral is supposed to confuse evil spirits.**

FAR LEFT **The view eastwards along the length of the nave looks even more impressive without chairs.**

LEFT Christ in Majesty is depicted in the carving in the tympanum above the Prior's Door. It is an outstanding example of the skill of a mid-12th-century stone-mason.

In the western corner of the transept a spiral staircase gives access to the Stained Glass Museum and is the beginning of the climb to the top of the west tower. The transept on the north side fell in the 17th century.

As you move into the body of the church it is worth making a diversion into the south aisle to see the Prior's Doorway. This gave access to the cloisters of the monastic church but after the dissolution of the monastery they were demolished and the door was left exposed to the elements for hundreds of years. Fortunately, the wonderful carving is now sheltered again. It dates from the mid-12th century, and the central tympanum has a magnificent Christ in Majesty, while the intricate work on each side

The lantern, built of oak, lead and glass, weighs 200 tonnes and is supported by means of a hammerbeam, a device apparently invented here and subsequently used to support the roofs of countless medieval churches. Angels decorate the painted panels below the windows, and at the centre of the ceiling a figure of Christ looks down on mortals below (see page 14). John of Burwell carved this wooden boss, receiving 2 shillings for his work, plus his keep at the Prior's table.

LEFT A glory of the lantern is that changing light reveals fresh beauty.

shows signs of the zodiac on the left with a miscellany of human activities on the right. Particularly amusing are the two men in a boat near the base. Each rows in a different direction!

From here return to the nave and walk towards the crossing. This is the glory of the Cathedral, a wide open expanse where the eye is led upwards by arch upon arch to the lantern – a fitting climax to one of the most imaginative and daring flights of human inspiration.

On 12 February 1322 the crossing tower, built two centuries earlier, collapsed bringing down much of the

LEFT One of the colourful angels supporting the hammerbeam roof of the south transept.

choir with it. Within six years it was replaced by an octagonal tower, which was crowned by the timber lantern in 1342, just five years before the Black Death brought building work to an abrupt halt. The structure is amazing in every sense – the idea of the tower and lantern came from the sacrist of the Cathedral, Alan of Walsingham, and not from a master mason (see panel opposite). The tower itself is a

ABOVE **A sinister Green Man lurks in the Lady Chapel.**

LEFT **The Lady Chapel was originally ablaze with stained glass that was smashed at the Reformation. The fragments that survived were later reassembled in the top part of this window.**

RIGHT **The RAF memorial window in the north choir aisle has a panel showing bombers flying over the Cathedral.**

complex-enough structure, its fluted columns rising past four vast Gothic windows and the great arches leading into the choir, the two transepts and nave. As the curve of the arches begins, the eight wooden fan vaults that support the lantern spring inwards towards its base. Alan of Walsingham gives his design a final daring flourish by offsetting the uprights and windows of the lantern with those of the tower.

Before moving forwards to the choir, it is best to look at the transepts at this point. The south transept is the oldest part of the Cathedral and dates from the first years of the 12th

ABOVE **This handsome cockerel is in Bishop Allcock's chantry at the end of the north choir aisle.**

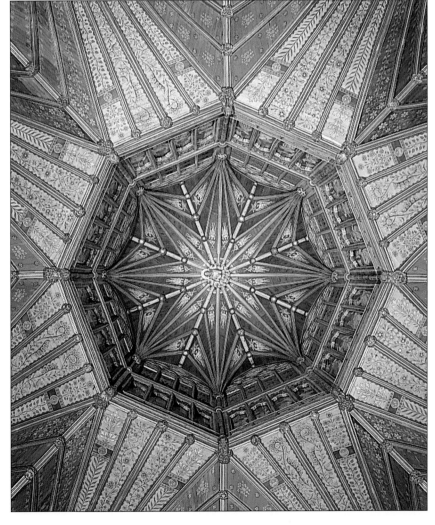

RIGHT **The spectacular view looking upwards from beneath the centre of the octagon.**

century, when St Etheldreda's shrine was moved into the new church. The early Norman work is striking in its massivity though later masons introduced increasingly florid decoration. This part of the building displays close parallels with the architecture of Winchester Cathedral, a consequence of Abbot Simeon having been Prior there before his posting to Ely in 1081. The north transept is slightly later in date, with subtle differences in style and detail. A door in its north-east corner gives access to the Lady Chapel.

Visitors entering the chapel from the gloom of the transept are stunned by its dazzling light. In medieval times the impact would have been even greater, with stained glass in the enormous windows and the countless

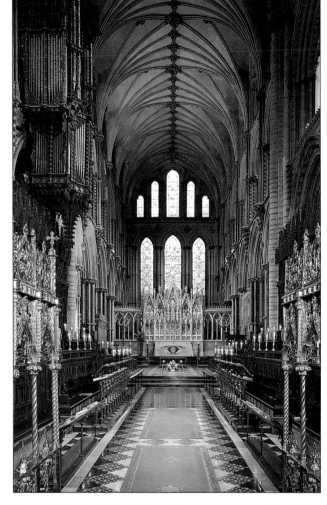

figures in their niches elaborately painted and gilded. The discoloured plain glass that succeeded it was recently replaced with splendid new lights, thanks to the generosity of industrial and private donors. This results in a sparkling new look for the magnificent chapel. It dates from 1321 but the fall of the crossing tower led to work being postponed until c. 1335, and it was only completed in 1353. The stone vaulting has a span of 46ft (14m), with its

Continued on page 18.

ABOVE The choir of Ely Cathedral, looking towards the site of St Etheldreda's shrine.

LEFT This carving of a peacock in the choir-stalls commemorates Dean Peacock, who was in office during the 19th-century restoration of the Cathedral.

A walk in Ely

This leisurely stroll takes little more than one hour. Start at Oliver Cromwell's House, just to the west of the Cathedral. The route skirts the Cathedral, passing by medieval buildings once part of the monastery. It then descends to the riverfront before returning via the Park with its Norman earthworks and wonderful view of the Cathedral. A visit to the latter can be made by entering through the west door and leaving by the south.

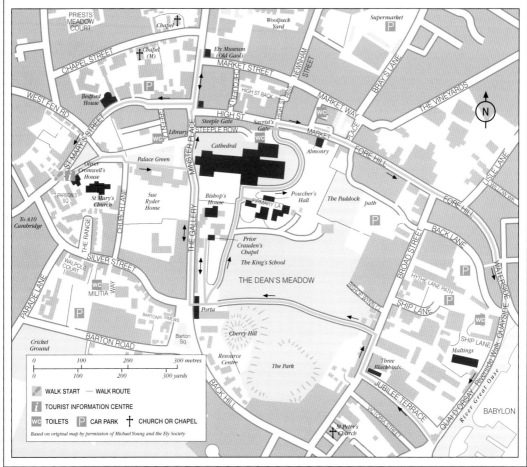

Based on original map by permission of Michael Young and the Ely Society

START at **Oliver Cromwell's House** (p.20) (*below*), where 'God's Englishman' lived for some ten years from 1636. It is now a museum and tourist information centre. Head towards the

Cathedral and pass **St Mary's Church** on the right. It dates from the 13th and 14th centuries and is Ely's parish church. Continue ahead to cross the Green and pass the **cannon** (*above right*) given

to the city by Queen Victoria after the Crimean War. Pause to admire the great west tower of the

Cathedral and the Galilee Porch. On the right is the former **Bishop's Palace** (*left*), now a Sue Ryder home, which largely dates from Bishop

16

Laney's time (1667–75) though there is also early Tudor work. Opposite, on the left of the Green, are two splendid Georgian houses. The one on the left is the **Chantry**, so called because it occupies the site of Bishop Northwold's chantry chapel.

Cross the road and, if you don't wish to visit the Cathedral, turn right down the Gallery (so called because a covered way once connected the Bishop's Palace to the Cathedral). Note the splendid Norman decoration of the west transept. A little further on there is a gateway giving a good view of the lantern and also of the bishop's residence, formerly the **great hall of the abbey** – its massive chimney has its own window! Although much altered over the

centuries it retains a 13th-century under-croft. Continue along the Gallery and pass through the **Porta** (*left*) on the left. Dating from 1396, it was the principal gatehouse of the monastery and now serves as the library of the King's School. To the right as you emerge from the gate is the **barn** of the monastery (now school refectory) but if time permits turn sharp left down a short cul-de-sac and see two relics of the medieval priory: **Prior Crauden's Chapel** is on the right, 'a gem of the Decorated style' dating from 1324 (see p.31 on admission). At the end of the lane, **Queen's Hall** faces you. It was built by Prior Crauden for the visit of Queen Philippa, wife of Edward III.

Return from the cul-de-sac and turn sharp left towards the Cathedral to admire another view of the chapel. **Priory House** (p.6), once the home of the prior, adjoins the chapel on the left.

Just before reaching the south entrance of the Cathedral, turn right down Firmary Lane, another cul-de-sac, taking its name from the vast infirmary of the monastery.

Powcher's Hall (*right*) on the left was part of this, while the **Black Hostelry** on the right was the guesthouse for Benedictines from

other foundations. Go back down the lane and bear right to walk around the east end of the Cathedral, noting the new **gargoyles**. Having

passed the east end of the Lady Chapel, turn right to leave the precincts via the **Sacrist's Gate**. Turn right into the High Street to walk past the medieval **Almonry**.

The High Street becomes Fore Hill at the Almonry Restaurant – which has a fine vaulted undercroft – and descends to the river. Keep ahead into Waterside, following the main road as it swings right. **Crown**

Point (*right*) is the twin-gabled house on the left where the road divides. Oliver Cromwell signed a document here in 1636. Pass the Antiques Centre and bear right at the river along Quayside. The narrow house on the right is the **Ladder House**, specially built for the ladders of a brewery that once stood close by. Pass the **Maltings** (p.24) and walk down **Quai d'Orsay** (Ely was twinned with Orsay in 1981) and at the Cutter Inn turn right away from the river up a footpath. At Broad Street turn right. The house on the corner (the **Three Blackbirds**, once a pub) is thought to be the oldest in Ely. Cross the road and look

for a castellated gate on the left into the **Park**. The pathway follows the edge of the Dean's Meadow and gives fine views of the Cathedral. To the left, atop **Cherry Hill**, are the remains of a Norman motte-and-bailey castle. Go back through the **Porta** and

retrace your steps along the Gallery to pass the west front of the Cathedral again. At the crossroads, with the **Lamb Hotel** on the right, you can either make a detour to visit the **Ely Museum** by going straight on past the hotel to the Old Gaol, now the museum, on the corner of Market Street, or turn left into St Mary's Street. **Bedford House**, on the right, was once the headquarters of the Bedford Level Corporation, whose coat of arms and motto (*below*) are

above the door ('Arridet arridum' means 'Dryness pleaseth'). A few steps further along this street of handsome houses and you are back at **Oliver Cromwell's House**.

ABOVE **Ovin's stone is the oldest feature of the Cathedral – an Anglo-Saxon monument to St Etheldreda's steward.**

centre being only 13 inches (33cm) higher than the sides – a particularly daring structure, again the inspiration of Alan of Walsingham. The Lady Chapel served as a parish church after the Reformation until 1938.

The presbytery of the Cathedral, the part to the east of the choir, was financed by Abbot Hugh of Northwold and was built between 1234 and 1252. Purbeck marble is used in the columns to contrast with the lighter stone of the arches right up to clerestory level. At the east end the eight slim windows (lancets) draw the eye towards the reredos and altar, added by Sir George Gilbert Scott as part of his

restoration in the mid-19th century. St Etheldreda's shrine with those of her sisters originally stood in front of the altar steps, and today a slate plaque flanked by candles marks its position. Scott also commissioned woodcarving for the choir-stalls, fortunately retaining the sixty misericords, where the medieval craftsmanship is one of the glories of the Cathedral. The choir aisles contain many interesting tombs and monuments with two chantry chapels. Bishop West's chantry, at the end of the south aisle, was completed just five years before the monks were forced to leave at the dissolution.

To view the exterior of the Cathedral and the remains of the surrounding monastery, it is best to leave through the south door, which leads into the remains of the cloisters through the beautiful Monks' Door (notice the famous gravestone beside this, dedicated to two railwaymen). The King's School, founded in 1541 as the Cathedral Grammar School, uses many of the surviving monastic buildings seen to the right as you walk away from the Cathedral. The Porta, the main entrance to the monastery, now serves as the

BELOW **The extravagant 16th-century vaulting of Bishop West's chantry chapel in the south choir aisle.**

BELOW **Most schoolchildren find a visit to the Cathedral exciting – here a group inspect the tomb of Sir Robert Steward (d.1570), a forebear of Oliver Cromwell.**

RIGHT **The intricate 12th-century stonework of the Monks' Door.**

school library. Instead of passing through the gate, bear left on the footpath that skirts the Dean's Meadow on the south side of the Cathedral. From here the great length of the Cathedral is apparent, and there are fine views of the lantern and west tower. The latter was originally topped with a spire but in the late 14th century the spire was replaced by an octagonal belfry 60ft (18m) high. This has proved to be an enduring problem as over the centuries the Norman foundations have shown themselves inadequate to support the additional weight.

RIGHT **The magnificent west tower of the Cathedral seen from near Priory House.**

BELOW **The Porta is the main gateway into the Precincts and now serves as the library for the King's School.**

Oliver Cromwell 1599–1658

The 17th century saw the resolution of conflict between monarch and state which had smouldered since the feudal society began to collapse with the advent of the Tudors. It could never have been expected that Oliver Cromwell, a humble fenland squire with a passion for religion and politics, would lead 'The Grand Rebellion' which toppled the King from the throne and set Cromwell in his place as Lord Protector.

Although not wealthy, Cromwell's parents were well connected, and he had cousins in many of the most powerful families in the land. A distant forebear was Thomas Cromwell, who dispersed the wealth of the monasteries in the reign of Henry VIII with a large proportion being diverted into his own coffers and those of his relations.

Oliver Cromwell was born in Huntingdon in 1599, attended Cambridge University, and in 1620 married Elizabeth Bourchier, daughter of a wealthy London merchant. They lived at Huntingdon, where he farmed and, probably, ran the local brewery. He soon became active in politics and was elected to Parliament in 1628. His upbringing had given him an enduring prejudice against the

LEFT **This portrait of Oliver Cromwell (a copy of one by Lely) shows the Protector at the height of his power. It is one of several paintings of Cromwell to be seen in Oliver Cromwell's House.**

BELOW **Oliver Cromwell's House also houses Ely's tourist information centre.**

Established Church and specially against the power held by the bishops. He also had an instinctive feeling for injustice, and in attempting to save commoners from being dispossessed by greedy landlords he made powerful enemies who removed him from Parliament and forced the family to leave Huntingdon for St Ives. Some of the gentry felt threatened by the ideas proposed by Cromwell, regarding him as a dangerous radical who wanted to do away with aristocracy, bishops, and even the King himself. The Cromwells moved to Ely on the death of Elizabeth's wealthy uncle Sir Thomas Steward in 1636. At this time Oliver appears to have been depressed and frustrated by the failure of his political work and was considering joining a Puritan colony in America.

Oliver and Elizabeth already had a large family so the small fortune they inherited was welcome. Cromwell resumed fighting for his religious beliefs and the welfare of commoners and became Member of Parliament for Cambridge in 1640. This gave him a platform to promote his radical policies, though it was his success in forming the New Model Army and

THE HOME OF OLIVER CROMWELL AND HIS FAMILY. CROMWELL ROSE TO POWER DURING THE ENGLISH CIVIL WARS, TO BECOME "LORD PROTECTOR OF THE COMMONWEALTH" DURING ENGLAND'S BRIEF PERIOD AS A REPUBLIC IN THE MID 17TH CENTURY. THE CROMWELL FAMILY LIVED IN ELY FOR SOME TEN YEARS FROM 1636 TO 1646.

leading it in battle that ultimately brought him power as uncrowned king between 1654 and 1658.

The Cromwells lived in Ely for some ten years but moved to London shortly before the Civil War. He probably disliked the affectionate nickname 'Lord of the Fens', bestowed on him by local people.

Museums and Attractions

FAR RIGHT This splendid panel is one of the major exhibits to be seen in the Stained Glass Museum. Made in 1927 for a Glasgow convent by the Irish artist Harry Clarke, it shows St Wilfrid, companion of Queen Etheldreda.

The city has three museums, two with distinctive themes, and the other dedicated to illustrating the development of Ely from prehistoric times to, more or less, the present day.

Oliver Cromwell's House stands by St Mary's Church on the Green. Originally built in the 13th century, it served St Mary's as a vicarage before becoming a museum and before that was a public house. Oliver Cromwell inherited the house from an uncle in 1636 and lived there for some ten years as a collector of tithes (see pp.20–21); his last two daughters,

RIGHT The reconstruction of a 17th-century kitchen in Oliver Cromwell's House.

BELOW A drawing depicting Oliver Cromwell's House when it served as an inn.

Frances and Mary, were born here. Apart from Hampton Court it is the only house that he lived in which survives. Visitors will find rooms arranged with furniture and artefacts of his time, and there are excellent audio commentaries, both on Cromwell and on the history of the fens. The rooms include the oak-panelled Parlour, the Kitchen, dating from 1215, Cromwell's Study, the so-called Haunted Room, the Portrait Room, and a Civil War Exhibition. The carefully restored house also serves as the tourist information centre.

The Stained Glass Museum occupies the southern triforium of the Cathedral, reached by a stairway in the west transept. The museum displays stained glass from all corners of Britain and illustrates how it is manufactured, a process that has hardly changed since medieval times. Examining the glass at such close quarters enables the visitor to

appreciate the extraordinary skill of the glass-painter and craftsman. A panel illustrating St Paul Preaching at Athens is a fine example, painted on to a piece of glass less than 2mm thick. One of the museum's recent acquisitions is a spectacular panel by the Irish artist Harry Clarke, depicting, appropriately for Ely, St Wilfrid, a great supporter of Queen Etheldreda.

The Ely Museum is located in Market Street and occupies the building which the bishop, the ultimate legal authority in Ely until 1836, used as a gaol. The museum has nine galleries which tell the story of Ely through the ages, from pre-historic times until the Second World War. One of the flint weapons on display attracts experts from all over Europe, and there is a splendid model of the Roman grange or procurator's house whose founda-tions were recently discovered at Stonea (see panel on page 4). The debtors prison and the condemned cell have been reconstructed to illustrate the terrible conditions suffered by prisoners in the last years of the bishop's rule.

ABOVE **Children on a visit to Oliver Cromwell's House enjoying them-selves by dressing up in period costume.**

RIGHT **The con-demned cell – a reconstruction at the Ely Museum.**

Shopping: For a city of moderate size Ely has a surprisingly wide range of shops. The main shopping centre is concentrated on the High Street and one of the two supermarkets is situated close by. The market-place remains a hub of Ely's commerce as it has done for centuries, though market-day was changed from Saturdays to Thursdays in 1801. The general market still flourishes on Thursdays with stalls selling a spectacular variety of local fruit and vegetables from the rich fen soil. There is now an additional market-day on Saturdays devoted to crafts, antiques and collectables.

Over the last 30 years or so Ely has become well known for its antique shops. The largest of these, which incorporates the showrooms of several dealers, occupies a former maltings on the Waterside (not to be confused with the Maltings itself, which is primarily a cinema, restaurant and leisure centre but also a regular venue for antique and craft fairs). There are antique shops in outlying villages as well, notably Burwell, Soham and Littleport.

ABOVE **Thursdays are the busiest day of the week at Ely with the market in full swing.**

RIGHT **Ducks are very demanding along Ely's river-front. The former maltings in the background is now an antiques centre.**

RIGHT The river is always busy with colourful cruisers in summer, and the pubs and restaurants are popular venues.

RIGHT AND BELOW The Hospital Carnival in May is an ever-popular event in Ely when inhabitants let their hair down to help the local hospital.

Eating out: Ely and its district offers a wide spectrum of menus from which to choose, be it in pub or restaurant. It is even possible to find eel offered in at least one establishment. Although beer is no longer brewed in the city, its pubs have an excellent selection of brews on tap, many of which will please the real ale connoisseur.

Entertainment: Throughout the year there are events for the concert-goer to enjoy, with the Cathedral

being the main venue. On six days of every week (except during summer holidays) evensong is sung in the Cathedral which presents English choral singing at its very best.

Events: The May Fair, held in Fore Hill car park, commemorates the death of St Etheldreda and has taken place since medieval times.

The Hospital Parade enlivens a Sunday in May and its colourful floats attract donations for local charities. In July the riverfront stages an Aquafest in which most participants suffer a soaking, while in August Ely celebrates the Great British Market Week.

The Fens and Surrounding Area

The magnificently preserved steam-engine at Stretham dates from the 1860s and is the only one of its type to survive. As the fens dried and sank, hundreds of wind-powered pumps were necessary to lift water into the rivers. However, these were inefficient at best and useless in calm conditions. Before the advent of diesel and today's electric pumps, the steam-engine was the first technology to offer a reliable way of pumping water, and it rapidly displaced the wind-pumps of the fens. The Old Engine at Stretham may still be seen working, though today it is powered by electricity and not steam.

The landscape of the fens is a direct result of their draining. The first **drainage work** in southern fenland was undertaken by the Romans. They wished to make it easier to move troops into potential troublespots and so constructed a gravel causeway west to east between Peterborough and Denver. They also straightened the courses of the rivers Ouse and Cam and dug many drainage dykes to enable more land to be cultivated. In their time the land was about 20ft (6m) higher than it is now, so the water drained from dyke to river by gravity; today the greater part of the fens lies 10ft (3m) or so below sea-level.

In Anglo-Saxon and early medieval times the wealthy monasteries concentrated on making water transport more efficient by straightening the river courses. The meandering Ouse was brought to Ely by diverting it between Stuntney and Quanea to make the transport of building materials easier as the walls of the Cathedral rose higher.

The landscape of the fens changed for ever when the Company of Adventurers, a syndicate led by Francis, 4th Earl of Bedford, raised money for drainage and hired

BELOW **Two views of the disastrous floods of 1947.**

RIGHT Flooded washlands in 1998.

Cornelius Vermuyden, a celebrated Dutch engineer, to plan and oversee the work. His design was based on shortening the course of the Ouse below Ely by 10 miles (16km) by digging a straight channel (the Old Bedford River) for 21 miles (34km) from Earith to Denver. Sluices controlled the flow of water at both ends, the one at Denver designed to prevent tidal water from flowing further upstream. This channel was completed in 1637 but the Civil War interrupted work on a parallel cut (the New Bedford River) and the sluice at Denver until Cromwell ordered the digging to resume. In 1651 the New Bedford was complete and the sluice at Denver began to operate.

The narrow strip of land between the Bedford rivers (Hundred Foot Washes) relieved pressure by being flooded in winter, and in summer cattle grazed its rich pasture. Local people were divided in their opinions about the work. Those employed on it were in favour, while those who still lived in the traditional fenland way, relying on fishing and wildfowl, were opposed.

Vermuyden's scheme relied on gravity and was never entirely completed. An unforeseen consequence of drainage was that the land rapidly began to sink as the fenland peat dried out. Also, cultivated topsoil, rich but light, was blown away by spring gales. Hundreds of wind-powered drainage pumps were built in an attempt to raise water from dyke to river. The advent of steam, diesel, and then electric pumps brought reliability and at first it seemed that they might succeed in preventing flooding, but when heavy rainfall or melting snow coincided with a high tide, as it did in the latter years of the 1930s and, worst of all, in 1947, it became apparent that flooding still remained a threat to the region. In 1964 a relief channel ironed out the meanders of the Ouse from below Denver to King's Lynn. Another cut-off channel flowing to Denver collects floodwater from the rivers Lark, Little Ouse and Wissey.

The **sluices at Denver** are at the heart of the Fenland flood protection system. Here information boards explain the scheme and outline the history of fenland drainage. Riverbank walks give wide views across land lying lower than the rivers.

BELOW An aerial view of Denver Sluice – the lynchpin of Fenland flood protection.

RIGHT **Pubs are an essential part of village life in the fens. This attractive thatched inn is on the village green at Wicken.**

BELOW **The drainage mill at Wicken, one of the most famous images of fenland.**

Prickwillow is the archetypal village of the Black Fens, with many of the houses overlooked by steep riverbanks. The Drainage Engine Museum impressively displays the enormous oil-fuelled engines that used to pump water from dykes to rivers. Other artefacts chronicle the struggle against flooding.

Wicken Fen is a tract of fenland that has remained untouched by drainage and agriculture. Visitors have a choice of routes into the heart

of a reedy wilderness, where bird-watchers are well catered for.

The Wildfowl and Wetlands Trust operate the nature reserve at **Welney**, which offers spectacular sights in winter with many thousands of waterfowl and swans finding sanctuary. Floodlights illuminate the feeding in the evening. In spring and autumn migrant waders and warblers visit Welney, and in summer there are thriving colonies of resident birds, butterflies and dragonflies.

The River Nene was diverted to flow directly to Wisbech from Peterborough but its former course is an attractive feature of the small market town of **March** (market-days are Wednesdays and Saturdays). St Wendreda's Church is famous for the 118 angels that embellish the double-hammerbeam roof. St Wendreda's is one of the churches featured in Dorothy Sayers' *The Nine Tailors*, a Lord Peter Wimsey mystery (see panel above).

Probably the most popular book to make the landscape of the fens a location is *The Nine Tailors* (1934) by Dorothy L Sayers (1893–1958). The author grew up at Bluntisham, the daughter of a country parson (her house is pictured above), and though her novel disguises locations by giving them fictitious names the atmosphere of the fens in the 1930s is well caught in this mystery tale featuring Lord Peter Wimsey and the bells of fenland churches (the Nine Tailors being the toll rung on the death of a parishioner).

LEFT **Racehorses returning from the gallops on Newmarket Heath.**

The old town of **Newmarket** was almost totally destroyed by fire in 1683, when it was already the centre of horse-racing in England. 'The sport of kings' has been centred on Newmarket ever since. Newmarket has two racecourses, about 2500 horses in training, and is the home of the Jockey Club, the National Stud and the National Horse-racing Museum.

Famous gardens surround the equally famous house of **Anglesey Abbey**, dating from 1600, which contains the Fairhaven Collection of paintings and furniture.

St Mary's in the village of **Burwell** is the Cambridgeshire church that most clearly rivals the airiness of the 15th-century 'wool' churches of Suffolk. The chancel is rich with angels, some holding musical instruments. **Burwell Museum** is centred on the windmill and illustrates life in the village.

Denny Abbey was founded in 1160 for Franciscan nuns but ten years later was given to the Templars, who used it as a sort of retirement home for their knights. Later it became a nunnery again before being adapted as a farmhouse after its dissolution. The Farmland Museum has interactive displays as well as workshops displaying country crafts.

Haddenham is a picturesque village grouped around a large church. Many of the houses have mansard roofs, giving them a continental flavour. Haddenham is the

ABOVE **Many fenland villages have attractive signs illustrating their history. The one at Soham is typical.**

highest fenland village, 120ft (366m) above sea-level.

Soham has a fine church, and its windmill is a notable landmark. A monastery was founded at Soham shortly before Etheldreda built hers at Ely, but when both were sacked by Vikings Ely was rebuilt and Soham abandoned. The Normans built a causeway to link the town with Ely, 5 miles (8km) to the north-west.

Tall towers of two medieval churches overlook the village of **Swaffham Prior**. St Mary's is the church used today; its octagonal Norman tower may have been the inspiration for Ely's medieval octagon. St Cyriac's was the rival church – its tower survives, dating from 1809. However, its unusual stained glass with First World War scenes was transferred to St Mary's.

There is a small but fascinating museum on the outskirts of Ely commemorating the bomber pilots and aircraft that flew from **RAF Witchford** and from neighbouring RAF Mepal, the headquarters of two famous New Zealand bomber squadrons.

LEFT **Denny Abbey was originally a Franciscan nunnery but later became a farmhouse.**

On the night of 2 June 1944 the first wagon of an ammunition train caught fire as it approached Soham station. The wagon was loaded with 500-pound (227kg) bombs and behind it there were another 50 wagons carrying similar loads. Both the signalman and the fireman died in the explosion while the driver of the train was hurled 200 yards (183m) by its force and survived. Many windows in Soham were broken and the explosion left a crater 15ft (4.6m) deep. The town would have been obliterated but for the bravery of the engine-driver and the fireman. All three men were subsequently awarded the George Cross.

Further Information

All details are correct at the time of going to press but please telephone to confirm opening times before making a visit.

Anglesey Abbey (NT)

Gardens and 17th-century house with the Fairhaven Collection of paintings and furniture; there is also a working watermill.

ABOVE **Anglesey Abbey dates from 1600 and occupies the site of an Augustinian abbey.**

Lode, Cambridge. Tel & fax: 01223 811200. www.national trust.org.uk/angleseyabbey. House open end Mar–Oct Wed–Sun and Bank Hols 13.00–17.00. Garden open end Mar–Jun Wed–Sun 10.30–17.30, Jul–Aug daily 10.30–5.30 (Thu 10.30–20.00), Sep–Oct Wed–Sun 10.30–17.30, Nov–Mar (part of garden only) Wed–Sun 10.30–16.30 or dusk if earlier. Mill open same days as garden but opening times 13.00–16.30; Nov–Mar Sat, Sun only 11.00–16.00. Admission charge.

Burwell Museum

Presentation of life in a fen-edge village; adjacent windmill.
Mill Close, Burwell. Tel: 01638 741512. mysite.freeserve.com/ burwell_museum. Open Easter Sun–last Sun in Oct Sun, Thu & Bank Hols 14.00–17.00. Admission charge.

Denny Abbey and Farmland Museum (EH)

Denny Abbey has an unusual history from 12th-century Benedictine monastery then Franciscan nunnery to 16th-century farmhouse. The farm buildings tell the story of rural life, with hands-on activities for children.
*Ely Road, Waterbeach.Tel: 01223 860489. Open Apr–end Oct 12.00–17.00.
Admission charge.*

Downfield Mill

A working windmill.
*Fordham Road, Soham. Tel: 01353 720333. Open Sun & Bank Hols 11.00–17.00.
Donations welcome.*

Ely Cathedral

*Tel: 01353 667735. Open in summer daily 07.00–19.00; winter Mon–Sat 07.30–1800, Sun 07.30–17.00.
Admission charge.*

ABOVE **16th-century decoration in Bishop West's chantry chapel, Ely Cathedral.**

Services: every weekday with Choral Evensong at 17.30 (said on Wed); Sun: Sung Eucharist at 10.30; Choral Evensong at 15.45.

ABOVE **The emblem of East Cambridgeshire District Council.**

Ely Museum

This museum relates the story of Ely and the Isle from the Ice Age to the present, including tableaux of the condemned and debtors cells. There is a rolling programme of temporary displays, talks and events.
The Old Gaol, Market Street. Tel: 01353 666655. Open daily except Christmas & New Year, summer 10.30–17.30; winter 10.30–16.30. Admission charge.

National Horse Racing Museum

The story of horse racing is told here, with hands-on galleries and a horse simulator.
99 High Street, Newmarket. Tel: 01638 667333. Open mid-Apr–Nov Tue–Sun 11.00–17.00 (10.00 on Race Days), also Mon in Jul & Aug. Booking preferable for groups. Admission charge.

National Stud

By going on a tour, you can find out all about the breeding and training of the thorough-bred stud.
*July Racecourse, Newmarket. Tel: 01638 663464. Tours daily Mar–Sep, also on Race Days in Oct & Nov Mon–Sat 11.15 & 14.30, Sun 14.30. Tour hotline: 01638 666789.
Admission charge.*

Oliver Cromwell's House

Oliver Cromwell lived in this now carefully restored house for some ten years from 1636; excellent audio commentaries. *29 St Mary's Street, Ely. Tel: 01353 662062. Open Apr–Sep daily 10.00–18.00, Oct–Mar Mon–Sat 10.00–17.15. Admission charge.*

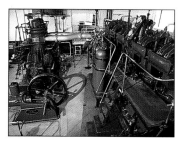

ABOVE **The impressive display of drainage engines at Prickwillow.**

Prickwillow Drainage Engine Museum

This pumping station was opened in 1831. Displays chart the draining of the fens since the 17th century, the effect of drainage on land levels and the workings of the modern drainage system. *Main Street, Prickwillow. Tel: 01353 688360. Open beg Mar–Apr & Oct Sat & Sun 11.00–16.00; May–Sep daily except Wed & Thu 11.00–16.30. Contact for details of special run days. Admission charge.*

Prior Cauden's Chapel

A perfect example of the Decorated style of architecture, built in 1324; the chapel is now used by the King's School. *Ely Cathedral precincts. Tel: 01353 662062. Key obtainable from Cathedral Admissions south door, or Dean and Chapter Offices, Firmary Lane, or from the Bursar's Office, The King's School, Barton Road Farm, during working hours.*

ABOVE **This dramatic painting by Graham Austin depicts wartime action over the city of Ely.**

RAF Witchford

Small museum commemorating the bomber pilots and aircraft that flew from here and RAF Mepal. *Lancaster Way Business Park, Ely. Tel: 01353 664934 or 666666. Open May–Sep Mon–Fri 10.00–16.30, Sun 10.00–16.30. Admission free.*

ABOVE **The pleasing interior of St Mary's Church.**

St Mary's Church

Ely's much-loved parish church stands close to the cathedral and dates from the 13th century. *St Mary's Street, Ely. Open during daylight hours and the usual services are held on Sun.*

Stained Glass Museum

This national collection traces the history of art from the Middle Ages to the present. *South Triforium, Ely Cathedral. Tel: 01353 660347. Open summer Mon–Sat 10.30–17.00, Sun 12.00–18.00; winter Mon–Fri 10.30–1630, Sat 10.30–17.00, Sun 1200–1615. Admission charge.*

Stretham Old Engine

Dating from 1831, this is the only water-pumping steam engine to survive from this era. *Stretham. Tel: 01353 649210. Open Good Fri–end Aug on 2nd Sun of month and Bank Hols 13.30–17.00. Admission charge.*

Tourist Information Centre

Oliver Cromwell's House, 29 St Mary's Street, Ely CB7 4HF. Tel: 01353 662062. www.ely.org.uk Open summer daily 10.00–18.00; winter Mon–Sat 10.00–17.15. Guided tours arranged.

Wicken Fen (NT)

A nature reserve of fenland with two waymarked trails. *Lode Lane, Wicken. Tel: 01353 720274. Visitor centre open daily 09.00–dusk (fen open dawn to dusk). Admission charge.*

Wildfowl and Wetlands Trust

Famous Welney nature reserve with its thousands of wintering swans and ducks. *Hundred Foot Bank, Welney. Tel: 01353 860711. www.wwt.org.uk Open daily except Christmas Day 10.00–17.00. Admission charge.*

Acknowledgements
Text by John Brooks.
The publishers wish to thank the Dean and Chapter of Ely Cathedral and Ely Tourist Information Centre for their valued cooperation in producing this book.
All photographs © Jarrold Publishing with additional pictures by kind permission of: Barry Aldritch, RAF Witchford: 31 (top); Cambridgeshire Collection, Cambridge Central Library: 6 (top right), 8 (centre), 26 (top right & bottom), 29 (top right); Cromwell's House Museum (photos by Jarrold Publishing): 20 (top), 21, 22 (centre & bottom), 23 (top); East Cambridgeshire District Council: 7 (bottom); Ely Museum: 4 (top), 23 (bottom); Environment Agency, Peterborough: 27 (bottom); The Stained Glass Museum Trust, Cambridge: 22 (top).

Printed in Great Britain.
ISBN 0 7117 1078 3   2/03

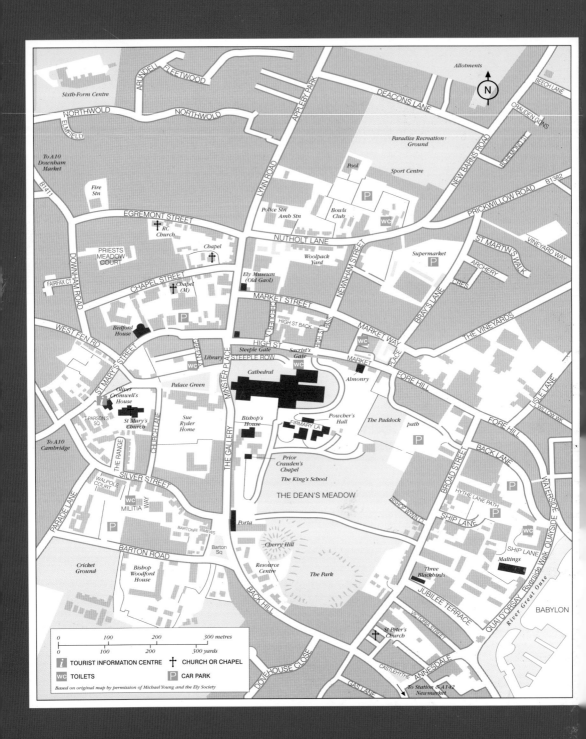

Allotments

N

Sixth-Form Centre

ARUNDEL FLEETWOOD

DEACONS LANE

BEECH LANE

CRAUDEN GDNS

NORTHWOLD NORTHWOLD

APPLEBY PARK

LYNN ROAD

Paradise Recreation Ground

NEW BARNS ROAD

ROBMOND

PRICKWILLOW ROAD

B1382

ELMFIELD

To A10 Downham Market

B1411

Fire Stn

Pool

Sport Centre

P

P

VINEYARD WAY

ST MARTIN'S WALK

EGREMONT STREET

RC Church

Police Stn Amb Stn

Bowls Club

WC

ARCHERY

CRES

PRIESTS MEADOW COURT

Chapel

NUTHOLT LANE

Woolpack Yard

Supermarket

P

DOWNHAM ROAD

FAIRFAX ROAD

CHAPEL STREET

Chapel (M)

Ely Museum (Old Gaol)

MARKET STREET

NEWNHAM STREET

BRAY'S LANE

FORE ST LANE

THE VINEYARDS

HIGH ST BACK

MARKET WAY

WEST FEN RD

Bedford House

ST MARY'S STREET

GREENS

P

Library

HIGH ST

Steeple Gate STEEPLE ROW

Sacrist's Gate

WC

MARKET

WC

FORE HILL

Oliver Cromwell's House

PARSON'S SQ

St Mary's Church

Palace Green

CHURCH LANE

MINSTER PLACE

Cathedral

Almonry

FORE HILL

LISLE LANE

WILLOW WK

THE RANGE

Sue Ryder Home

THE GALLERY

Bishop's House

FIRMARY LA

Powcher's Hall

The Paddock

path

P

BACK LANE

WATERSIDE

To A10 Cambridge

SILVER STREET

Prior Crauden's Chapel

The King's School

BROAD STREET

HYTHE LANE PATH

P

WALPOLE COURT

WC

MILITIA

WAY

THE DEAN'S MEADOW

JUSTICE WIND NG

P

SHIP LANE

WC

PARADE LANE

BARTON'S MEWS

Barton Sq

BARTON ROAD

Porta

Cherry Hill

BACK HILL

Resource Centre

The Park

Three Blackbirds

Maltings

SHIP LANE

QUAY D'ORSAY

Riverside Walk

QUAYSIDE

River Great Ouse

Cricket Ground

Bishop Woodford House

JUBILEE TERRACE

VICTORIA STREET

BABYLON

0   100   200   300 metres
0   100   200   300 yards

St Peter's Church

DOVE HOUSE CLOSE

CASTLEHYTHE

ANNESDALE

GAS LANE

To Station & A142 Newmarket

i TOURIST INFORMATION CENTRE   **†** CHURCH OR CHAPEL

WC TOILETS   **P** CAR PARK

Based on original map by permission of Michael Young and the Ely Society

JARROLD
publishing

ELY

ISBN 0-7117-1078-3

9 780711 710788